Beautiful Life..
Because Ugly Didn't Win
A Wing and A Prayer

D1714209

Written by Shannon Higgins
With Kimberly Mucker-Johnson

Qui Docet Discit Publishing, LLC
Louisville, KY 40272
quidocetdiscitpublishing@gmail.com

DEDICATION

First giving honor to my Lord and Savior Jesus Christ from whom all of my blessings come from. Also, I dedicate this book to the ones that were always there for me and the ones that were not. The ones that believed in me and the ones that did not. The ones that supported me on this journey called Life and the ones that put obstacles in my way. Throughout this process, the Word has taught me to love those that hate me and do good to those that despitefully use me. With that, I bless everyone and I present this book as sacrifice of praise.

-Shannon

CONTENTS

CHAPTER 1

I CRIED, HE HEARD

"When my father and my mother forsake me, then the LORD will take me up.."
–Psalm 27:10

It was Thursday, September 23, 1982, at the

University of Kentucky Medical Center in Lexington,

Kentucky when I was born. I was told at 6:04 PM, I

exited the womb of my sixteen-year-old mother,

Tammy. According to my life book, she gave me two

very special things – the beautiful name of Shannon and

the gift of life. Those two things would be the only

things that she would give me. They would be the two

things that I would cherish my entire life.

Although I have never had a heartfelt talk with

Tammy, I am left with the impression that my birth

probably interrupted her life of drugs and the streets.

Tammy was a troubled youth and had been in and out of

foster care. I guess she was unstable and could only

duplicate the instability that she had experienced

herself. Tammy floated from place to place so she

didn't know or understand what it meant to have

stability, what it meant to have a home. Bedsides,

Tammy wasn't but a child herself and she had no idea of

what she was going to do with a child. This child called

Shannon.

Since I don't have all the details, I can only speculate

that Tammy must have been in and out of abandoned

buildings all the time. These deserted buildings must

have been the places that she slept at, ate at, and fixed

at. I wonder if she felt safe in darkness. People tend to

hide things in darkness. I wonder if she hid me in one of

those abandoned buildings, forgot where she left me

and couldn't find me. I have always pictured that she

looked and looked for me, but just couldn't find me. But

maybe that's just a fantasy. Maybe she had no intention

of coming back to get me. All I know is that on Day 2 of

my life, Tammy left me. She left me in one of those

buildings. Alone. For two days, I cried without any

response from anyone. I fidgeted as I laid in my soiled

diaper. Too small to escape the grasp of hell. I had no

other choice but to keep crying. I was hungry and no

one fed me. I was thirsty and no one gave me milk. I

was lonely and no one comforted me. There was no one

to get warmth and comfort from. You know, the basic

needs of any newborn baby. I was **ABANDONED.** I was

left behind.

From that day to this one, the thought of how she

could have forgotten about me has crossed and recrossed my mind millions of times. I only find solace in the fact that a man found me and took me to a safe place. I have forgiven Tammy because she was probably high or intoxicated, so she did not understand what she was doing. The safest place in the whole wide world is in the hands of God. By the grace and mercy of God, an angel found me and took me to my auntie's doorstep.

My auntie fought for custody of me, but the legal system would not allow it. She battled the court system for years, but was denied because she could not obtain the consent of my mother or father. My mother was nowhere to be found and my father was in the streets or in and out of jail, so he wasn't stable enough to care for me or to give consent. After years of trying to find my mother and setting up appointments that she never honored, they turned me over to foster care. I became a

ward of the state.

There is a song that often comes to my mind when I

think about this part of my life. It goes like this...*I love*

the Lord, he heard my cry and pitied every groan. Long

as I live and troubles come, I'll hasten to his throne.

PRAYER PAUSE

Dear Heavenly Father,

Bless the soul that is reading these words. Even though, they may not be able to express how they are feeling or what they are going through, Lord you know. Let my story serve as a testimony to them that you will never leave nor forsake your children. Even when it seems as if they are lonely, Lord let them know that you are there for them. You will take them up! Thank you, Lord for being a God that can be touched by the feelings of our infirmity. Thank you, Father for understanding our moans and groans. Thank you, Lord for not leaving us to die in our own dirty soil. In the name of Jesus Christ, Amen.

CHAPTER 2

LOST, FOUND AND LOST AGAIN

"To everything there is a season, and a time to every purpose under the heaven: A time to be born, and a time to die; a time to plant, and a time to pluck up that which is planted..."

-Ecclesiastes 3:1-2

First I went to a transitional home with a pastor and his wife. You see In foster care, you go to transitional homes until they find a suitable home for you. I was a visitor in many such homes and experienced traumas from some of my visits. For example, one man abused me because I had a hard time learning to use the potty. Now that I look back, I believe that it took me longer to do some things because I was going from place to place so much. Whenever you move, you have to learn new rules and ways of living because the last family does things differently than the current family. I think this was the reason that I had a hard time learning new skills such as using the potty. He would spank me really hard whenever I peed on myself, so eventually the state took me out of his home. The thing about it is, Ms. Karen, his wife never did anything to help me. She just allowed him to beat me.

Next, I stayed with an elderly couple. This was only for a short term because they were not really equipped to take care of a toddler. Eventually the state found me a family.

Now, I had a daddy, a momma, and two brothers. My daddy was a pastor of a church in another county and he worked at the Dare to Care Food Bank. Momma was an Orthopedic  secretary at a doctor's office. Before adopting me, they had adopted two boys that became my two brothers. I was the only girl and the baby. I felt special. I was three years old when I became a Higgins. We lived a normal, stable life. I finally learned what the word "family" meant.

About two years later, Momma was diagnosed with cancer, but we, kids were not told. We did know that she was sickly because she would stay in the bed all the time, which was unusual for her because we were an active family. I remember how we would pile into Daddy's old style camper and go to the Smoky Mountains. Or we would ride to different places in Daddy's little Tempo. I would be sandwiched between my big brothers in the back seat. Even people from my daddy's church would travel with us sometimes, but the sicker Momma became, the less we traveled. It seemed like our family began to fall apart.

Momma just couldn't do even simple things anymore like walk to the store, 41st Street Market. Momma used to play the piano at church before she got sick. She even got Brother Joe to give me piano lessons because she believed that as a member of the first family, you have to be able to do all kinds of things for the church. After she took ill, I never finished those lessons. She didn't have the strength to make sure that we stayed active.

Daddy's church was in Campbellsburg, KY and we would ride there every Sunday. Also, when special events such as Campbellsburg Day came up, we would go. In fact, that is exactly where we were when the Deacon got the call. That particular year, Daddy had one of the deacons to escort us to Campbellsburg Day since Momma was too sick. I would learn later that while we were there, my daddy called the deacon and told him that our momma had passed away. I didn't understand, but my brother tried to explain that something happened to Momma. When we got back home, Momma was not there and we wouldn't see her again until the funeral. After the funeral, we would never see her again. It all happened almost in slow motion. First, we were a family that went everywhere and did everything together. Then Momma was not able to do even the simplest things like braid my hair. I remember my auntie would come over to braid my momma's hair and my hair. Next, she stayed in the bed more and more. Then, she was gone...forever. The cancer had spread and they couldn't stop it. I was eight years old when my momma died of cancer. I had a momma for five years.

My momma must have been popular because it seemed like they shut down the whole city for her funeral. I know they, at least, shut down the office where she worked, so that they could all attend the funeral at Shiloh Baptist Church. We were going to have the funeral at our church in Campbellsburg, but the church was too small for all the people that wanted to pay their respects because like I said my momma was popular. She had lots of friends, sisters and stuff. Plus, she was a good woman and that is what they all kept saying at the funeral...*She was a good woman.*

After losing my birth mother, then finding a family only to lose another momma I must have been devastated. But following in the steps of my brothers, we did not drop a single tear. When I go back in time, I keep going back to that day when the deacon dropped us off. I remember my daddy was sitting on the same bed where Momma had spent many sick days. My brothers and me climbed onto his lap and he told us that she was gone. I never released that pain not even at the funeral. I remember at the funeral many people cried and I even saw Daddy crying, but me and my brothers did not shed a single tear.

Not long after the funeral, Daddy took us to Disney World because he wanted to get away for a while so we could grieve. At least that's what he said, but for some reason we never released. Disney World was just another trip except this time Momma wasn't with us.

I guess eventually life goes on because many women started liking Daddy. I think they wanted to be his first lady. He began dating women and it wasn't long before he found a new woman and I found myself without a family again.

PRAYER PAUSE

Dear Heavenly Father,

We know that there is a season and a time for every purpose. Father, we don't always know or understand your season or purpose, but your Word tells us that all things are working together for the good of them that love you and are called according to your purpose. Lord, help us to praise you even when adversities are birthed into our lives and when it looks as if our blessings are dying. Help us to trust you enough, so that when you plant us in good ground one season and then pluck us up the next, we won't lose faith. Lord, we want our attitude and deposition to always bring glory and honor to your name. We trust you, Lord, to always do good towards us throughout our lives. In the name of Jesus Christ, Amen.

CHAPTER 3

OUT OF CONTROL BEHAVIOR

"For God hath not given us the spirit of fear; but of power, and of love, and of a sound mind ."

-2 Timothy 1:7

I don't know exactly when it happened, where it happened, why it happened, or how it happened but I found myself back in group homes. I vaguely remember there came a season when Daddy couldn't or wouldn't take care of three children on his own. I have secretly thought that he wanted to start a new life and we wouldn't be a part of that new start. I am sure by now you realize that there are so many unanswered questions in this story. That's because it is a reflection of my life...the topsy, turvy life of Shannon. My life has so many unanswered questions, so many unfulfilled promises. There are some questions I have managed to find answers to and then there are other questions I have been trying to find answers to throughout my entire life. So here I was under state custody again going to group homes and this time they attached the label, **OUT OF CONTROL BEHAVIOR** onto me.

I am not going to lie, I had episodes of acting a "fool". Now that I am in social work, I believe that I must have been overwhelmed by all that I had been through and I guess I just couldn't take it anymore. Everybody has a breaking point.

I would run away. I would steal. I wouldn't stay in school. I wouldn't obey those that had authority over me. Many social workers didn't want my case because they didn't want to have to deal with my unruly behavior. I was too much! I was out of control! I attended Eastern High School along with other kids from the group home and there were days that we would just decide not to go to school. We would just leave the school and run away. Eventually I became so depressed that I was suicidal.

Although they tried, Seven Counties' Extended Care Unit was not able to curb my suicidal tendencies. Perhaps, because I refused to take my medication. But I only refused because they all had side effects that only made me feel worse. Seroquel made me like a zombie. Depakote made my hair fall out. And Trazodone made me only good for sleeping. They were not helping. They were smothering me. They were killing me softly. Eventually when they ran out of options of how to deal with me, they sent me to Carl D. Perkins Job Corp near Ashland, Kentucky. This place was so far away that I had to stay because there was nowhere to run. It was in the middle of nowhere. Since I was there, I thought I should learn something, so I managed to acquire some skills in retail sales.

Years later, I found out that Momma had left me some money, but Daddy had used all of that money to get help for me. It must have hurt him to see me sink to such low levels.

PRAYER PAUSE

Dear Heavenly Father,

Sometimes we don't know how to deal with this thing called Life. Instead of coming to you for assistance, we take matters into our own hands and it ends up a mess. Lord, today I stand before you because I have created a mess of my life. In fact, I have made my bed in hell and there is not anything on this earth that can get me out. I have tried medications, drugs, sex, boyfriends, disobedience, stealing, and even attempted suicide...none of it worked. I need help and I now realize that only you can help me. I am calling on your name this day as my source, my only source in the name of Jesus Christ, Amen.

CHAPTER 4

STIPEND OR RECOMMITMENT

"If any of you lacks wisdom, let him ask God, who gives generously to all without reproach, and it will be given him."
-James 1:5

After years of driving adults crazy, I finally turned 18. My social worker presented me with a choice -- take $200 stipend or recommitment (stay in a group home until I was twenty-one). It didn't take me but a few seconds to make my decision...I wanted my freedom. I did not want to be in state custody anymore. I did not want to be told when to go to sleep, when to wake up, and when to eat. "Give me the $200 stipend", I retorted. I had finally reached adulthood and decided that I could parent myself (after all, this journey has mainly been solo). Besides, I just wanted my freedom. My social worker stalled on the money until after she had a brief discussion with me. She said that most people that come from a group home end up pregnant, end up on the streets, or end up in jail. Her comment did not convince me to recommitment, however her analysis must have been correct because I ended up on the streets and eventually I ended up in jail.

I started off taking my $200 to Kentucky State University (this was the first college I attended). Luckily when you have been a ward of the state, they pay for your college education. *Side note: I recommend that anyone that is a ward of the state to take advantage of the opportunity to a free college education.* The issue with me was the fact that I was only able to make it through one semester at Kentucky State University because freedom was a huge responsibility that I wasn't prepared for. I ended up not going back after Christmas break. I resented the fact that I didn't have any parental support like other college students. No one sent me care packages. No one helped me. No one seemed to care.

I often found myself going to visit other students' family during breaks. One time, I went home with my roommate to visit her family. It felt good to belong and to be welcomed to a family gathering. Anyways, the state does not prepare you to survive on your own. Their system is a system of dependence. You learn to depend on them for everything. They tell you where you are going, when you are going and what time you will be there. Pretty much everything is organized and structured for you. When you leave there, you have no idea of how to be self-sufficient. Nobody trained me to live on my own. Nobody showed me how to live independently. I didn't have a mother, daddy, or anyone to teach me. I had to do everything by myself and for myself. If I didn't know that I was supposed to do something, then it didn't get done and I suffered the consequences. I had to schedule my own classes, which was difficult. Everything was so difficult because I had no idea of what I was doing. I just didn't have...I just didn't have anybody to tell me to get up on time, get to class on time, or manage my money. Not being prepared for independence is a cruel lesson to have to learn solo.

Surviving is always first and foremost for me, so I knew that I had to come up with a new plan. I knew in order to survive that there were certain things that I had to do. College had provided me with my own place and with checks that I could spend on anything I wanted. It didn't click that I needed to maintain my academics in order to maintain my freedom. I was too engrossed

with my place, my money, and my survival. Academics

was left out of the survival equation, so I ended up

where I didn't want to end up – ground zero.

PRAYER PAUSE

Dear Heavenly Father,

Your Word tells us that if we don't have wisdom that we can come to you and you will give us what we need. This chapter of my life provides an example of someone that is lacking wisdom. Lord, I didn't know that I could count on you to provide my every need. The person reading this prayer and silently speaking these words into their own life may be lacking something that only you can provide for them. Lord, open their knowledge and understanding of you. Give them wisdom, so that they will come to your throne for their "lackings" and Lord, we thank you in advance for your goodness. In the name of Jesus Christ, we pray. Amen.

CHAPTER 5

FITTIN' IN

"O wretched man that I am! who shall deliver me from the body of this death?"
-Romans 7:24

If I had known that I would end up at ground zero ,
then I would not have done the things that I did. It all
began when I discovered some of my biological mother's
relatives. I had family that I could visit. I went to stay
with my mother's sister and her children. My older
cousin was cool and I enjoyed just hanging with her. In
fact, I enjoyed it so much that I decided that I wouldn't
go back to college. This cousin hung in the streets and I
wanted to be like her. I wanted to fit in. I soon learned
that my cousin was a booster, someone that steals. We
began stealing from Dillard's at Bashford Manor Mall.
She was my teacher and she was so good at boosting
that she would save bags from the store that she was

stealing from and use them for her stolen goods. But before placing them in the bags, she would wrap the goods in aluminum foil – that way if it had one of those little alarm tags on it, then the aluminum would block the system. Once we got the goods home, she knew how to burn those tags off. I quickly learned this whole process because I saw it as an opportunity to get things that I felt like I needed. I remember one time we stole Tommy Hilfiger everything -- shirt, pants, shoes, and sweaters. Stealing became a way of life for us. We would go in a store and steal something just to get an outfit to wear to the club for one night and that would be it. I was DRESSED. I was happy because I felt good about being with family and looking good.

UNTIL...we started getting caught. The first time I was caught, they put me in a shoplifting diversion class.

I remember them saying, "We are going to put you into this little class. You complete the class then we'll take it off your record...just don't do it again". Of course, I didn't listen to them. When I finished the class, we started stealing more frequently and started getting more stuff. The truth is I don't know what I was thinking. It wasn't long before we got caught at Target.

They took us to the back of the store. Inside the office, they questioned us and called the police. When the police got there, we were handcuffed. They took us out of the store in handcuffs. It seemed as if everyone in the store just stopped and stared at us. It was real embarrassing. I went before the judge and was charged with shoplifting. My punishment was...60 days of home incarceration. Do you think I did as I was told? NO! I claimed to value my freedom so much, but on New

Year's Eve I decided to take the watch off. I wanted to go to the club with my cousin. We danced and had a good time. After our partying, we went back to my auntie's house. My auntie said the police had been there looking for me. It wasn't long after she had spoken those words that the police were banging on the front door. They arrested me. This time, the judge decided that I would have to do 90 days in jail because I had "escaped". I had never been to jail before. For 90 days long, I lived at ground zero. I saw some of the same people get locked up, released, and locked up again. It was like a revolving door. It was crazy. It was depressing. It was torture. I knew that I did not ever want to have to go there again.

I don't see my cousin anymore because we have two different lifestyles. My cousin will never try to live a different life. But as for me, I knew that I had to live

differently.

PRAYER PAUSE

Dear Heavenly Father,

I realize that you know all and you see all. I stand before you naked and ashamed of how I have disobeyed your Word so many times. I love and appreciate you because you see me as I am and yet you still love me. In fact, you love me so much that you sent your only begotten son, Jesus Christ to die on the cross for me. For this, I love you even more! Your Word says in Luke 12:48: "For unto whomsoever much is given, of him shall be much required: and to whom men have committed much, of him they will ask the more." Lord, you have given me so much and while I realize that I could never repay you for the ransom you provided, I can feed your sheep. Much is required of me and all I have is a testimony. A testimony to other lost and hurting souls that do not know of your goodness. Help me to be a living testimony of your love. Allow others to see your light shining through the brokenness of my life. Allow others to see your love even though I am not always "good". I thank you for sending your son as the ultimate sacrifice for someone such as this wretched soul called me. In the name of Jesus Christ, I pray. Amen.

CHAPTER 6

PILLAR TO POST
"...if I make my bed in hell, behold, thou art there."

-Psalm 139:8

I don't know the background of where the phrase
"pillar to post" came from. In fact, I always thought it
was from "pillow to post" because that's what I thought
I heard people say. Despite the origin of such a phrase,
the point of the matter is I found myself homeless. I
found myself living from pillow to post. Basically, there
were two shelters that I called home, the Salvation
Army, which at the time was on Brook Street and
Wayside Mission, which used to be on Market Street.
This was a pattern for me at least a couple of years --in
and out of homeless shelters -- from "pillow to post". I
carried my clothes in black trash bags and dragged them
from pillow to post. Sometimes people would let me

34

stay with them for a while. Sometimes I would sleep in the car. Oftentimes, I would end up back at one of the two shelters. This was my lifestyle. This was how I lived.

The thing about my living arrangement was that I was never raped. I was never attacked. I was able to sleep, get up and wash up every single day. Life at the shelter was arranged like one big dorm room filled with rows of beds. If one shelter was full, then you would have to check another shelter for a bed. There were times when there weren't any beds available and those were the times when I had to make other arrangements like a car, someone's house, or outside. At the shelters, there were many women and children. It makes you wonder where are all the men. The shelter was full of bed bugs and lice. Shelter workers clean as much as possible and even the people staying there clean, but people are not as clean as they can be because of their situation. Every morning you have to spray your mattress down with Lysol Disinfectant because you might not get the same bed -- that's not promised to you. People steal so you have to sleep with your purse under your pillow. It's a hard life because different people have different things going on. They may snore, talk in their sleep, and some of them were just plain crazy. In fact, some of them did not have access to their meds, so there is a possibility that they might stab you or anything. I mainly kept to myself and I kept my mouth shut.

Most days, to keep myself occupied, I filled my time with trying to find a job. I made sure that I washed my clothes at the shelter and if you are a "resident" at the shelter for a long time, then they will put you in a program where you can actually leave your clothes

there. That way, if you are searching for a job or

working, you won't have to carry black trash bags

around with you. All the while I was living like this, I

kept in the back of my mind that I had a goal. My goal

was that I refused to spend my entire life like this.

PRAYER PAUSE

Dear Heavenly Father,

Life happens to all of us and there are times when we find ourselves - physically or spiritually in a place that feels like hell. It is at these moments that we tend to do a lot of self-reflection because we are wondering if this will last forever. Discouragement tends to run rampant during these situations and at times we want to just give up. Lord, the only thing we have is your Word. In your Word, it says..."if I make my bed in hell, then you are there." Thank you for being there for my "hell bed" moments. I love you ad adore you because you truly are LOVE. In the name of Jesus Christ, AMEN.

CHAPTER 7

ENTRAPMENT

Stand fast therefore in the liberty by which Christ has made us free, and do not be entangled again with a yoke of bondage.

-Galatians 5:1

Living at the shelter was not much different than some of the other bad situations in which I found myself. Nor was God any different in this case, he rescued me. I finally got out of there! I got my own place. A place I could call "home". But I never took on the attitude that I was better than the ones that didn't make it out. I remember going back to Wayside to volunteer. I took a group of students from Boys Haven with me and I couldn't help but notice that many of the same people were still there. This revealed two things to me – not everyone makes it out and the shelter has some type of attraction that entraps you (if you let it). The shelter will serve you three meals a day. They offer a Day Room where you can stay until 5 pm and then go to the dorm to sleep. They don't require you to go and find a job. In other words, if you become satisfied with their offerings, then you can get trapped. You'll end up there for your entire life, which is entrapment.

As soon as I was able to find a job, I went to work. I started off working at Labor Ready. During my time there, I met many people that were homeless, mentally unhealthy, or both. Labor Ready is not the sort of place that you plan to work at for the long term, but they are a resource to help you get on your feet. The good thing about them is they transport you to the job location and pay you the same day. That's pretty much it. When I was working there, I knew why I was working there. My goal was to pay my bills, so I didn't have to be homeless.

I had rent, LG& E, and phone. I didn't want to go back to the shelter, so I was going to do what I had to do.

Not too long before the writing of this book, I saw one of the guys that I worked with at Labor Ready. I saw him walking the streets and then on another day, he was sitting outside of Dollar Tree. He was looking kinda rough with his backpack so I stopped.

I said, "What are you doing? You don't work for Labor Ready no more?"

He said "Well I gotta get a haircut and I got to get some more steel toes they broke."

I remember thinking to myself that he had too many excuses for not working. Therefore, he must be entrapped with homelessness. He was entrapped. The next time I saw him he was sitting over at Thornton's on Bardstown Rd. I asked him if things going better now. He still looked rough and downtrodden as he mumbled,

"No". I offered to take him to the shelter. He said "Naw". He didn't want to go. I don't understand why people wouldn't continue to work for Labor Ready, especially if they are homeless. This guy could be like me by using Labor Ready as a stepping stone to get his own place.

Even though, I have had my own place for years now and I work in a satisfying career as a social worker, I don't turn my nose up at the homeless because I have not forgotten that at one time I was one of them. Also, in the streets and shelters are some special people and you would be surprised if you listened to their stories. Their stories are extraordinary!

PRAYER PAUSE

Dear Heavenly Father,

The birth, death, and resurrection of your son, Jesus Christ has set me free. And whom the Son sets free is free indeed! Lord, I thank you for my freedom. I thank you because when I was entrapped, you gave me the ability to get free again. Lord, I know that you are not like us. You don't have favorites or respect of persons, so what you did for me I know you will do for others. I ask that you will give any person that is entrapped, the knowledge, understanding, and wisdom they need on how to live free. And Lord once you show them how to be free, help them not to become entrapped again. In the name of Jesus Christ, AMEN.

CHAPTER 8

LEMONS INTO LEMONADE

Ye shall not *need* to fight in this *battle*: set yourselves, stand ye *still*, and see the salvation of the LORD with you...

-2 Chronicles 20:17

After all I had been through, I needed a place to feed my spirit, so I began attending a church. But after being baptized and committing to a ministry, it became one of the worst experiences I've ever had to survive. I almost threw my life away dealing with the wrong pastor, associate ministers, and church members. What should have been a ministry of love and faith turned out to be a ministry full of gossip and hate. I personally witnessed manipulation from the pulpit. Not to mention, I ended up being ostracized because they lied on me. These false prophets were claiming to be one thing when they were just the opposite.

The great thing about me is that I am an observant person. The degradation that I witnessed from the pulpit was enough to make anyone deny the faith and give up on God. Who would have thought that I would have to fight to survive in the church? But God, who is rich in mercy, gave me the strength to make it through. I survived this rejection and now I am at a church where I am accepted. The pastor, associate pastors, and church members are not perfect, but they are humble, God-fearing people. Again, I win! I turned lemons into lemonade.

PRAYER PAUSE

Dear Heavenly Father,

I have been in some places and expected to find you. Lord, you were not there, but I didn't give up on looking for you. Lord, I need for your Word to be true and every man's word to be a lie. I need to know that you have my back in times of trouble because I know if you have my back then I can do all things through Christ who strengthens me. Thank you for teaching me not to become anxious in times of adversity. Thank you for teaching me to stand still and wait on your salvation. Lord, I love and adore you in the name of Jesus Christ, AMEN.

CHAPTER 9

I AM THE CHAMPION

And we know that all things work together for good to them that love God, to them who are the called according to *his* purpose.

-Romans 8:28

As of now I realize that only God has kept me while I am on this journey. This book only gives snippets of my experiences. You would be surprised of the journey I've traveled and places I've had to survive. We all have experiences in life, some good and some bad. Life is hard, and things don't always go as planned. During those moments you have a choice to make, you can either give in to the circumstances or use those experiences, as life lessons and overcome them. When negative events become learning opportunities, they make you a stronger person. Our life lessons are one of life's most valuable teachers because they show us ourselves, teach us about life, and show us our possibilities.

I've learned many things on this journey called Life. I've finished my first book, conquered a master's degree, started on another master's degree and developed the beginning stages of my own business. I've been able to overcome many tests and trials. Today, I realize I'm a CHAMPION!! I've been able to beat those who tried to beat me. Now I clearly understand that I don't need to look to others for approval.

As we drift through life, some of us are a little more focused than other. We tend to use the feedback from those surrounding us as our barometer as to whether or not we are actually successful. Looking to others for approval, whether it be in a professional world, on a project, or personally only leads to their opinions becoming your reality. I refuse to allow someone's opinions to dictate my life!

Today I have chosen to celebrate every win, big or small. I know that success breeds success. Rather than just being "celebrated" for showing up, make sure that you recognize and feel the value in your wins. I've also decided to move ahead and make sure that my life lessons are remembered as teachers that have shown me who I am and who I can be. Reflections should be done daily not once a year or now and then. When we don't reflect daily, we miss out on the opportunities that those experiences bring to us. Those stories that we interact with on a daily basis can be an inspiration and the groundwork for us becoming better human beings both personally and professionally. There is nothing worse than going through a difficult time in your life and feeling like it was a complete waste of effort.

Adversity has a way of defeating us and making us feel used up, but somewhere inside, we want to be able to make sense of our difficulties. We want to make them count for something positive. We have to know that all the pain we endured wasn't for nothing. I used to think adversity was something I had to suffer through to experience happiness. Hoping it wouldn't come, I avoided adversity, for the most part. But it always did. And it came with a force. Years of depression and unhappiness about the unknown and the abandonment left me feeling defeated and broken as a young adult. I wasn't sure how to deal with it. I was often angry, defensive, and in survival mode most of the time. Somewhere along my journey, I realized something very important. If I could find a way to change my perspective of pain and defeat, then the pain and defeat itself would change. I found a new way. It's called a different perspective. Sometimes, another perspective is all it takes to give you fresh eyes on your obstacles. Instead of my childhood being something I had to get through, I saw it as a necessary step for me to become the person I was meant to be. Without every aspect of the experience, I wouldn't have the capacity to be the real me -- full of flaws while at the same time full of victory. Those 10 years of abuse are now something I freely talk about. It's has become an advantage. If you are ready to turn adversity on its head, remember that what you are going through right now is temporary and has an expiration date. Your difficulties are the anchor to charting a new course in your life full of promise and purpose. Adversity is your greatest teacher working for you, and the more you can see the benefit that results from it, the more positive and good you will find in it. What better way to reach the next level of your life than to turn your adversity into your advantage. In my mind, I understand now that Life is not happening to me, but it is happening for me. Once I changed from "to" to "for", my adversity became my ally, no longer an enemy. I began to use my fears as a launching pad for the kind of person I wanted to become. Now, adversity is happening for me so that I can be the best inspiration for others. So that I can transform my mess into my mission. I AM THE CHAMPION!

PRAYER PAUSE

Dear Heavenly Father,

Lord, your Word says to count it all joy when I fall into diverse troubles because the trying of my faith worketh patience. So, I am not supposed to react to trouble like people who don't know you react. For me, I should rejoice because I know that these are the building blocks of becoming more than a conqueror. I thank you, Lord for every mountain you brought me over. For every trial, you saw me through. I thank you, Lord because you have made me into a CHAMPION. I pray the contents of this book serve as a testimony of your goodness. And Lord because you first loved me, I am going to spread the gospel by using my life as a living testimony. In the precious name of my Lord and Savior, Jesus Christ. AMEN.

ABOUT THE CO-AUTHOR

Dr. Kimberly Ann Mucker-Johnson met Shannon Higgins when Shannon came to Waggener High School and told her story. Dr. Mucker-Johnson believed that this story needed to get out to the masses because of the powerfulness of how Shannon overcame many obstacles and still maintained her faith.

As an educator for over 15 years, Dr. Kimberly Mucker-Johnson has witnessed first-hand the devastation that obstacles present in the lives of young people. She currently serves as an Instructional Coach, which has broadened her awareness of not only the obstacles at one school, but across an entire urban school district. In addition, she is currently working on a degree and state licensure in mental health counseling. She has facilitated presentations on resilience, which she strongly believes is a missing link in the lives of many minority youth. Like the examples given in this book, Dr. Mucker-Johnson believes that resiliency can be learned and when it is learned then today's youth become today's champions, they transition from victim to victor. While the story told in this book belongs to Shannon Higgins, Dr. Mucker-Johnson contributed to Shannon's story by adding the relevant scriptures and prayers that was the source of Shannon's breakthrough.

Dr. Mucker-Johnson lives in Louisville, Kentucky. She is married to Eric and has two sons, Derrick and Keonte'. Her list of accomplishments were not possible without many of her own obstacles and her faith in her Lord and Savior, Jesus Christ.

57771256R00036

Made in the USA
Charleston, SC
21 June 2016